SCHOLASTIC

11+ HOME TUTOR

AGES 10–11

GL Assessment

Verbal Reasoning

Explanation Practice Test

Published in the UK by Scholastic, 2026

Scholastic Education, Scholastic Distribution Centre, Bosworth Avenue, Tournament Fields, Warwick CV34 6UQ

Scholastic Ireland, 89E Lagan Road, Dublin Industrial Estate, Glasnevin, Dublin, D11 HP5F

A CIP catalogue record for this book is available from the British Library.

ISBN **978-0702-33670-6**

Printed by Bell & Bain Ltd, Glasgow.

MIX
Paper | Supporting responsible forestry
FSC® C007785

The book is made of materials from well-managed, FSC®-certified forests and other controlled sources.

1 2 3 4 5 6 7 8 9   6 7 8 9 0 1 2 3 4 5

www.scholastic.co.uk

For safety or quality concerns:
UK: www.scholastic.co.uk/productinformation
EU: www.scholastic.ie/productinformation

Author
Alison Milford

Editorial team
Rachel Morgan, Vicki Yates, Kate Baxter, Julia Roberts and Jennie Clifford

Design team
Andrea Lewis and QBS Learning

Illustrations
QBS Learning

p4 (blank crossword) Becris/Adobe Stock; p4 (play crossword) mynamepong/Adobe Stock; p4 (pile of books) Darwin Mulya/Adobe Stock; p4 (headphones) Oleksandr Panasovsky/Adobe Stock; p4 (book) Arash Design/Noun Project; p5, 6, 8, 11, 13, 15, 17, 19, 21, 23, 25, 26, 29, 31, 33, 35, 37, 39, 41, 43, 45, 47, 49, 51, 52, 55, 57, 59, 61 (pencil) Misturi/Noun Project; p6, 43, 55 (speech bubble) Napish/Noun Project; p6, 9, 10, 12, 14, 16, 18, 20, 24, 27, 30, 32, 34, 36, 38, 40, 42, 43, 44, 46, 48, 50, 52, 54, 58, 60 (lightbulb) Davo Sime/Noun Project; p6, 10, 12, 16, 20, 21, 24, 28, 32, 36, 40, 43, 44, 48, 54, 58 (girl character) Tana-mame/iStock; p8, 26 (letters) Widyatmoko/Noun Project; p9, 21, 27 (cogs) Iqbl Taufiq Alim/Noun Project; p9, 14, 18, 22, 26, 27, 30, 34, 38, 46, 50, 53, 56, 60 (boy character) Tana-mame/iStock; p10 (plant) Salman/Adobe Stock; p10, 12, 14, 16, 18, 22, 24, 28, 30, 32, 34, 36, 38, 44, 46, 54, 56, 58, 60 (magnifying glass) Liam Mitchell/Noun project; p10 (flowers) pingebat/Adobe Stock; p10 (toy car) PikePicture/Adobe Stock; p10 (wind blowing trees) Саша Мельник/Adobe Stock; p12 (eyes) Authay/Adobe Stock; p14 (opening door) Flash Vector/Adobe Stock; p14 (globe) hanohiki/Adobe Stock; p16 (music) Graficriver/Adobe Stock; p18 (horse and foal) Julia Anisimova/Adobe Stock; p18 (pen) Studio Zenith/Adobe Stock; (scissors) zaie/Adobe Stock; p20 (clock) ankomando/Adobe Stock; p20 (brain) Aiden Stonehouse/Noun Project; p20 (magnifying glass) Creative Stall/Noun Project; p21 (trees) MALAI Studio/Adobe Stock; p27 (dog) Stockgiu/Adobe Stock; p28 (hen) Anna Syvak/Adobe Stock; p38 (peach) uiliaaa/Adobe Stock; p38 (scarf) Wanicon/Adobe Stock; p40 (eyelash) Moschiorini/Adobe Stock; p42 (padlock) Design Queen/Noun Project; p44, 53, 56 (frog) Tamim 99Graphics/Adobe Stock; p48 (wind) Peterdraw/AdobeStock; p52 (maths symbols) SAMYA/Adobe Stock

Contents

Extended answers with explanations can be found online at www.scholastic.co.uk/pass-your-11-plus/extras/gl or via the QR code.

About Verbal Reasoning and the Tests

What is Verbal Reasoning?

What is verbal reasoning (VR for short)? Well, 'verbal' means 'to do with words', and 'reasoning' means using 'problem-solving and logic skills'. Verbal reasoning tests ask you to answer questions using your skills and knowledge of word structures and patterns, vocabulary, and sorting out reading information. Verbal reasoning also uses alphabetical codes and number patterns and rules. This book is going to be your guide to making sense of them all.

Verbal reasoning question types can look confusing and difficult to understand at first. You may find some of them easier to work out than others. However, by spending time before the tests getting to know each question type and trying out practice questions, you can become a verbal reasoning whizz-kid!

What Do I Need to Know and How Can I Improve My Skills?

To answer verbal reasoning questions with confidence, you need to have really good vocabulary skills. Here are some ideas for how you can boost your vocabulary to help you tackle the 11+ tests:

- One of the best ways is by reading lots! Both fiction and non-fiction will help you. Reading a variety of materials like books, newspapers and magazines can help you understand new words in different contexts. If it's written down and you're reading it, it will help you!
- Listening to podcasts or audio books can also help, especially if you pause to write down any words you don't understand and look them up in a dictionary.
- Playing word games such as board games, crosswords and word puzzles are a fun way to improve your word skills.
- Creating a journal of new words and their definitions.
- Making flashcards of new words that you can test yourself with later.

About this Book

This book will guide you through the different verbal reasoning question types one by one. It will explain everything you need to know and give you plenty of opportunities to practise what you've learned. It's like having your own tutor at home, ready to help you!

You'll find that the book is divided into chapters, each covering related question types:

- Word Meanings
- Reading Comprehension
- Making Words
- Codes
- Maths Skills

About the Chapter

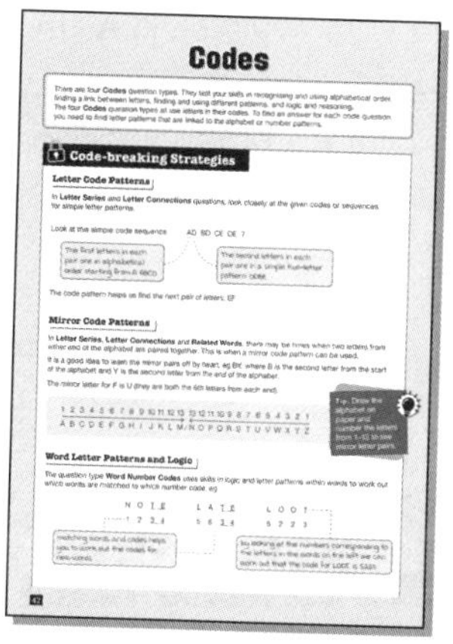

At the start of each chapter you'll find two pages giving some general information about the skills you need to tackle this category of question.

There are some 'Give it a Go' questions in this section which are designed to check that you've understood what's been introduced. You can find the answers to these questions at the back of the book.

Exploring the Question Type

Next in each chapter there is a page that guides you through answering some questions that are very similar to the test questions.

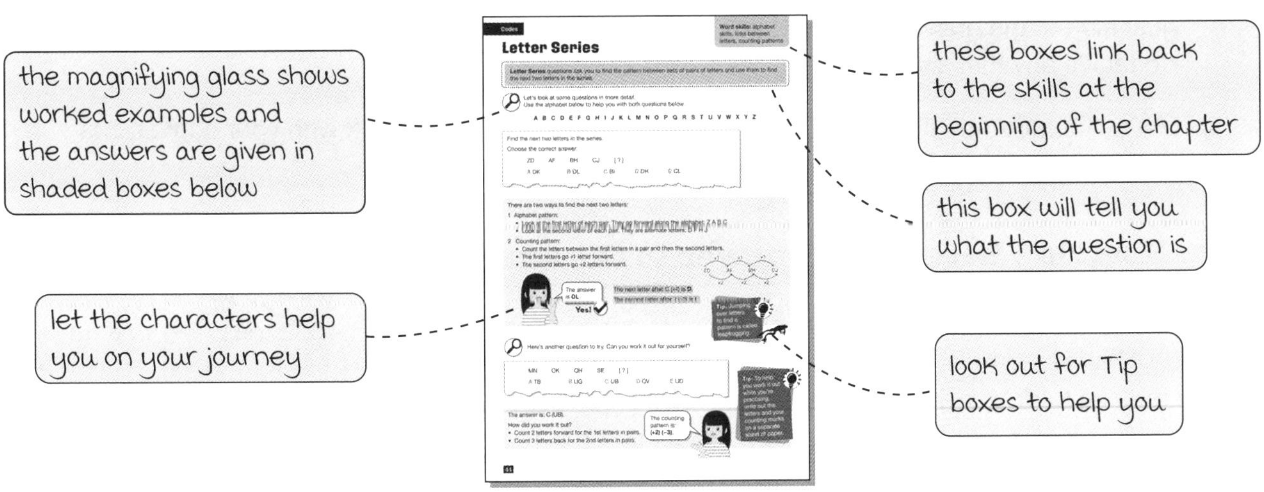

Let's Practice!

For each question type there is a page of practice questions, similar to those you might encounter in the test, to practise your understanding. If you get stuck, refer back to the previous page or look at the extended answers provided online.

Practice Test

At the end of the book, you will find a short practice test, do this at the end under test conditions. Look at your results, do you need to go back and practise a question type more?

Verbal Reasoning Top Tips

As you go through this book, you will pick up lots of tips and suggestions. You may even find your own ways of doing the questions which work for you. Here are a few to get you going!

- Double check your answers before writing them down.
- If you are stuck with a question, move on and return to it later.
- Have fun exploring words in thesauruses and dictionaries.
- Increase your logic skills with puzzles such as crosswords, code breakers, wordsearches.
- Find and list common letter patterns regularly used in some of the question types, for example ea, ow, sh.
- Eliminate any answer options you know are wrong and concentrate on the remaining options. This is helpful if you're a bit stuck.
- For tricky practice questions, looking at the answers will help you to understand how to work out the question so you'll be able to tackle similar questions next time.
- Don't try and do too much in one go. Short, focused sessions of 10-30 minutes feel manageable and are likely to be the most productive.

What Happens in the Test?

In the real test, you will be given just a pencil and a rubber, but that is all you will need. Always make sure you follow the instructions of the teachers leading the tests. You will be given a selection of different VR question types, this means that some types you see in this book will not be tested in your particular test – it is just luck of the draw! But if you are familiar with a wide range you should be able to tackle any that are included.

As testing arrangements vary across the country, it is best to check with your admissions authority or school if you have any specific queries.

How Do I Record my Answer to the Questions?

You will be given an answer sheet to write your answers on which will have a number of little boxes for each question. All you need to do is to draw a line through the box for the correct answer.

The answer sheets get read by computers, so keep your lines straight and clear to avoid confusion. You can colour in the whole box if you want, but time is short, so a line will do. If you change your mind, rub out the line and put a new, clear one in the box you have chosen. Do not write anything else on the paper, it will only confuse the computer that marks it! Tell your teacher at the end of the test if there is anything that you feel needs to be made clearer – they should be able to help you.

While this book doesn't have separate answer sheets, we have included the answer boxes for every question in the margin so you can get used to using them for your answers. In the test all of these answer boxes will be together on a separate sheet – so make sure you check the question numbers.

Tip: You can write on the question paper to help you work out the answer but you must record your answers on the answer sheet.

Progress Tracker

Keep track of your learning. Tick when you have completed the learning for each section and record your marks when you have completed each Let's Practise! section.

		Learning	Let's Practise!
Word Meanings	Similar Meaning	☐	/7
	Closest Meaning	☐	/6
	Opposite Meaning	☐	/6
	Two Odd Ones Out	☐	/7
	Word Connections	☐	/6
Reading Comprehension	Comprehension: True or Untrue?	☐	/3
	Comprehension: Most or Fewest?	☐	/3
Making Words	Make a Word	☐	/7
	Complete the Word	☐	/7
	Insert a Letter	☐	/7
	Move a Letter	☐	/7
	Hidden Words	☐	/7
	Missing Words	☐	/7
	Joining Words	☐	/6
Codes	Letter Series	☐	/7
	Letter Connections	☐	/7
	Related Words	☐	/7
	Word Number Codes	☐	/6
Maths Skills	Complete the Calculation	☐	/7
	Number Series	☐	/7
	Letters for Numbers	☐	/7
	Related Numbers	☐	/8
	Practice Test		/29

Word Meanings

There are five **Word Meanings** question types. These questions test your skills in understanding, recognising and using different word types, synonyms and antonyms, word groups and recognising connections between words.

Aa Word Skills

Recognising Types of Words

We use words all the time for reading, writing and talking. Each word can be sorted into a word types, which are called parts of speech.

Word Meanings questions focus mainly on these three types of words: nouns, verbs, adjectives. A few questions may also use adverbs, for example, 'soon', 'early', 'now', 'above', 'below'.

Word type	Examples
Nouns (n) – naming words	Common nouns: teacher, square, lion, cave Abstract nouns: education, health, pollination
Verbs (v) – action words	begin, destroy, explain, move
Adjectives (adj) – describing words	happy, vast, difficult, ancient

Tip: Knowing a word type can help you work out a word meaning and its connection with other words.

Recognising Word Groups

Word groups are words that have links with each other, for example words to do with transport, the ocean, school, holidays. The list is endless! They are used in question types such as **Two Odd Ones Out** and **Similar Meaning**.

GIVE IT A GO! Match the group name at the top to the word lists at the bottom.

words for angry | weather words | types of walking

rain snow wind sun | stroll march amble hike | furious mad enraged cross

Find three new words for these word groups:

outer space | types of running | types of cake

Tip: Have fun learning word groups by doing wordsearches, crosswords, creating word group posters or writing lists.

Knowing Synonyms, Homonyms and Antonyms

Most of the **Word Meanings** questions focus on word connections using synonyms, homonyms and antonyms.

Synonym

A word that has a similar or the same meaning:

- 'tired' is a synonym for 'sleepy'

Question type: You'll be looking at synonyms in **Closest Meaning** questions.

Homonym

A word that has the same spelling or sound but a different meaning:

- ring (n): band around finger
- ring (v): to make a clear sound

Question type: **Similar Meaning** questions are all about homonyms.

Antonym

A word that has the opposite meaning of another word:

- 'clean' is the antonym of 'dirty'

Question type: **Opposite Meaning** questions focus on antonyms.

Tip: A thesaurus is a great resource to find synonyms. Some list antonyms too.

Logic and Reasoning Skills

It can help to know words and their meanings but what if you read a word and don't know what it means or how it is connected to other words? Don't worry!

The tests also want you to use your thinking skills to work out words that you are not sure of by using clues connected to them. Here are a few tips.

- Focus on the words that you *do* know to help you work out the meaning of a word you don't know.
- Then look at the unknown word and say the word in a sentence.
- Make a reasoned guess.

- Read the question instructions slowly.
- Note the important words in bold or in capital letters.
- Look carefully at the example and pay attention to how the answer was found.

Think about or say the word in a sentence if you're unsure of a word and its connections.

Let's look at the question types in more detail.

Similar Meaning

Word skills: synonyms, homonyms, word groups, types of words

Similar Meaning questions ask you to choose one word that can be linked to two pairs of words that are in brackets.

Let's take a look at some questions in more detail.
In this question, there are two pairs of words.

Just **one** of the five given answers will go well with **both** of the two pairs of words.

Find the word and choose the correct answer.

(bush flowers) (scatter sow)

A wheat B plant C dig D rose E spade

first pair of words
second pair of words
five possible answers

- Look at the first pair of words. 'Bush' and 'flower' name things that grow; they are nouns.
- Compare this to the answer options. The words 'wheat', 'plant' and 'rose' work well. They are nouns and are things that grow.
- Now look at the second pair of words. The words 'scatter' and 'sow' are verbs.
- The words 'plant' and 'dig' work well with 'scatter' and 'sow' and they are also verbs.

Both a bush and flower are a type of **plant**.

We scatter or sow seeds when we **plant** them.

Let's do one more. Try to work it out for yourself.

(breeze gale) (wrap twist)

A storm B loop C wind D rope E tornado

Tip: If you are not sure of a word, say it in sentences to help you. Remember, two words might look the same but be spoken in different ways.

The answer is: C (wind).

How did you work it out?

- 'Storm', 'wind' and 'tornado' go with 'breeze' and 'gale'. 'Loop', 'wind' and 'rope' go with 'wrap' and 'twist'. The only word that goes with both pairs is 'wind'.
- It is a noun when it goes with the first pair and a verb when it goes with the second pair.

LET'S PRACTISE!

In questions 1–7, there are two pairs of words.

Just **one** of the five given word answers will go well with **both** of the two pairs of words.

Find the word and mark the correct answer in the box on the right.

1 (friendly considerate) (type sort)

A generous B mix C kind D gentle E variety

2 (chime peal) (band circle)

A ring B buzz C loop D bell E arena

3 (instruct teach) (engine locomotive)

A drill B carriage C line D train E tutor

4 (soar glide) (insect bug)

A flutter B fly C bee D wing E swoop

5 (elevator crane) (raise hoist)

A heave B pulley C lift D climb E stair

6 (looking glass reflection) (copy mimic)

A shiny B match C identical D polish E mirror

7 (stone boulder) (sway swing)

A rock B pebble C roll D cliff E wobble

Closest Meaning

Word skills: synonyms, word groups, types of words

Simple Meaning questions ask you to choose one word from a list of five words that can be linked to two pairs of words that are in brackets.

Let's look at two examples.
In this question, the two groups of words in the brackets are linked to the senses.

Find **two** words, one from each group, that are **closest in meaning**.

Choose **both** correct answers:

(look smell noisy) (touch sour stare)

A look X touch

B smell Y sour

C noisy Z stare

two groups of words

choose a word from each group that are similar to each other

- Read the words in both brackets. They are words linked to the senses.
- Let's look at the words in the first bracket. Both 'look' and 'smell' are sense verbs or nouns and 'noisy' describes a loud sound.
- Now look at the words in the second bracket. Both 'touch' and 'stare' are also sense verbs or nouns and 'sour' describes a taste.
- The words 'look' and 'stare' both describe the action of seeing. They are the closest in meaning.

The answer is **look** and **stare**.

Look at that eagle!

I am going to **stare** at the clock until it is time for the party.

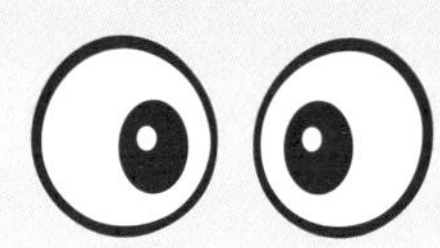

Here's another question to try. Can you work it out for yourself?

(road travel bus) (ticket street station)

A road X ticket

B travel Y street

C bus Z station

Tip: Remember to look for two words that are synonyms.

The answer is: A (road) and Y (street).

How did you work it out?

- In the first bracket, 'travel' and 'bus' could be linked to 'ticket', 'street' or 'station' but they do not have the same meaning.
- However, both 'road' and 'street' describe places for vehicles to travel on.

We drove down the **road**.

The bus moved slowly up **street**.

LET'S PRACTISE!

In questions 1–6, find **two** words, one from each group, that are **closest in meaning**.
Mark **both** correct answers in the box on the right.

1 (angry glum rude) (excited happy cross)

A angry
B glum
C rude

X excited
Y happy
Z cross

A B C X Y Z

2 (above behind on) (ahead over by)

A above
B behind
C on

X ahead
Y over
Z by

A B C X Y Z

3 (discuss shout announce) (debate sob sigh)

A discuss
B shout
C announce

X debate
Y sob
Z sigh

A B C X Y Z

4 (ruby jewel brooch) (diamond necklace gem)

A ruby
B jewel
C brooch

X diamond
Y necklace
Z gem

A B C X Y Z

5 (fire hot burn) (cold scorch light)

A fire
B hot
C burn

X cold
Y scorch
Z light

A B C X Y Z

6 (leap float soar) (crawl flutter pounce)

A leap
B float
C soar

X crawl
Y flutter
Z pounce

A B C X Y Z

Word skills: antonyms, word groups, types of words

Opposite Meaning

Opposite Meaning questions ask you to read two groups of words in brackets. Then find two words from each group which have the opposite meaning to each other (antonyms).

Let's get to grips with this question type by looking at examples similar to those you might find in the test.
In this question, there is a mix of nouns and verbs.

Find **two** words, one from each group, that are the **opposite in meaning**.

Choose **both** correct answers.

(door entry shut) (key open fasten)

A	door	X	key
B	entry	Y	open
C	shut	Z	fasten

two groups of words

choose a word from each group that are similar

- Let's focus on 'door' in the first bracket. Look to see if any of the three words in the second bracket are its opposite in meaning.
- Do the same with 'entry' and then 'shut'.

The only words that are opposite are **shut** and **open**.

Yes!

Shut the door!

Open the door!

Let's try another one. See how you get on by yourself.

(ocean hill city) (grass water land)

A	ocean	X	grass
B	hill	Y	water
C	city	Z	land

Tip: The vertical word lists may be an easier way to compare the words in each group.

The answer is: A (ocean) and Z (land).

How did you work it out?

- Start with the first word, 'ocean' and compare it to the other words: 'grass', 'water' and 'land'. The ocean is made of water, so it can't be that and grass grows on land, but ocean and land are opposites.
- Check the other options with 'hill' and 'city' to be sure.

Boats sail on the **ocean**.

Cities are built on **land**.

LET'S PRACTISE!

In questions 1–6, find **two** words, one from each group, that are the **opposite in meaning**.

Mark **both** correct answers in the box on the right.

1 (compete victory loss) (race prize defeat)

A compete X race

B victory Y prize

C loss Z defeat

A B C X Y Z

2 (tight mean squeeze) (plenty loose close)

A tight X plenty

B mean Y loose

C squeeze Z close

A B C X Y Z

3 (carry lift pick) (catch drop throw)

A carry X catch

B lift Y drop

C pick Z throw

A B C X Y Z

4 (angry explode wild) (tame burst weak)

A angry X tame

B explode Y burst

C wild Z weak

A B C X Y Z

5 (rain wet muddy) (puddle fog dry)

A rain X puddle

B wet Y fog

C muddy Z dry

A B C X Y Z

6 (combine instruct make) (separate join leave)

A combine X separate

B instruct Y join

C make Z leave

A B C X Y Z

Two Odd Ones Out

Word skills: synonyms, word groups, types of words

Two Odd Ones Out questions ask you to work out how three of the five listed words are connected. You can then find the two remaining words that are the odd ones out and not linked to the other words.

We can see how the questions work by looking at some examples.
In the question below, all the words have something to do with music.

Three of the five words are connected.

Find the **two** words that are **not linked** with the three words.

Choose the correct answers.

drum	choir	tuba	harp	dance
A drum	B choir	C tuba	D harp	E dance

word choices

you need to choose two options for this question

- Let's slowly read each word and compare them with the other words.
- Which three words have a strong connection?
- The words 'drum', 'tuba' and 'harp' are connected. They are all musical instruments.
- The words 'choir' and 'dance' are not musical instruments. They are the two odd ones out.

A **choir** is a group of singers.

People **dance** to music.

Here's another question to try. See if you can find the answer yourself.

carrot	melon	green	banana	plum
A carrot	B melon	C green	D banana	E plum

The two answers are: A (carrot) and C (green).

How did you work it out?

- The three connected words are 'melon', 'banana' and 'plum'. They are all types of fruit.

Tip: Focus on one word at a time to find any possible links with other words.

LET'S PRACTISE!

In questions 1–7, three of the five words are connected.

Find the **two** words that are **not** linked with the three words.

Mark **both** correct answers in the box on the right.

1 gallop trip sprint dash slip

A gallop B trip C sprint D dash E slip

2 alert weary dozy lively tired

A alert B weary C dozy D lively E tired

3 jellyfish octopus sand seaweed seahorse

A jellyfish B octopus C sand D seaweed E seahorse

4 clog hat boot sandal glove

A clog B hat C boot D sandal E glove

5 torch candle switch lamp plug

A torch B candle C switch D lamp E plug

6 waterfall camel cactus river sand

A waterfall B camel C cactus D river E sand

7 little petite colossal mini humongous

A little B petite C colossal D mini E humongous

Word Connections

Word skills: synonyms, antonyms, word groups, types of words

Word Connections questions ask you to choose one of the three words in each of the two brackets so that the sentence explains the connection between the two words in bold.

Let's look at some questions in more detail.
In this question, the first bracket lists words linked to sheep.
The second bracket list words linked to horses.

Choose the **two** words, one from each group, that will help the sentences make sense.

Choose **both** correct answers.

Sheep is to (lamb flock wool) as **horse** is to (trot foal neigh).

A	lamb	X	trot
B	flock	Y	foal
C	wool	Z	neigh

first set of words to choose from

second set of words to choose from

choose one from each set of words

Let's focus on finding a connection between a word in the first bracket and a word in the second bracket:

- The word 'lamb' and 'foal' have a connection. They are both baby names for the words in bold:
  sheep – lamb   horse – foal.
- The other words in the first bracket are not connected.
  First bracket: 'flock' is a group of sheep, 'wool' is a sheep's fur.
  Second bracket: 'trot' is a way a horse moves, 'neigh' is a sound a horse makes.

Sheep is to lamb as **horse** is to foal.

Try this question by yourself.

Write is to (draw pen story) as **cut** is to (scissors chop bandage).

A	draw	X	scissors
B	pen	Y	chop
C	story	Z	bandage

Tip: Read the sentences aloud to make sure the connection makes sense.

The answers are: B (pen) and X (scissors).

How did you work it out?

- Both a 'pen' and 'scissors' are tools for the verbs 'write' and 'cut'.

LET'S PRACTISE!

In questions 1–6, choose the **two** words, one from each group, that will help the sentences make sense. Mark **both** correct answers in the box on the right.

1 **Foot** is to (boot nail toe) as **hand** is to (hold finger wave).

A	boot	X	hold
B	nail	Y	finger
C	toe	Z	wave

A B C X Y Z

2 **Cold** is to (ice hot winter) as **fast** is to (slow jet quick).

A	ice	X	slow
B	hot	Y	jet
C	winter	Z	quick

A B C X Y Z

3 **Helicopter** is to (fly cockpit rescue) as **barge** is to (canal pull float).

A	fly	X	canal
B	cockpit	Y	pull
C	rescue	Z	float

A B C X Y Z

4 **Erupt** is to (volcano explode lava) as **shake** is to (crush earthquake flatten).

A	volcano	X	crush
B	explode	Y	earthquake
C	lava	Z	flatten

A B C X Y Z

5 **Three** is to (trio triangle number) as **yellow** is to (colour lemon sun).

A	trio	X	colour
B	triangle	Y	lemon
C	number	Z	sun

A B C X Y Z

6 **Glum** is to (feeling miserable angry) as **cheerful** is to (surprise sad jolly).

A	feeling	X	surprise
B	miserable	Y	sad
C	angry	Z	jolly

A B C X Y Z

Reading Comprehension

There are two **Reading Comprehension** question types: **True or Untrue** and **Most or Fewest**. Both question types ask you to find the answer from a set of information in sentences. Each question type tests your comprehension skills and abilities in examining, interpreting and sorting information.

Comprehension Skills

Examining and Interpreting Information

The **Reading Comprehension** questions are like a puzzle, with each sentence giving you a different piece of information. You need to use your comprehension and logic skills to help you to see the complete picture and then work out the correct answer.

When you look at a set of information:

1. Examine what information is being directly given to you.
2. Interpret and deduce what the information does not directly tell you.

Tip: Read each sentence twice to help you focus on the information.

Let's read through these information sentences:

- Aiza, Frankie and Mo go to gym club every Wednesday.
- Gym club always starts at 4.30pm.
- Frankie can often be up to five minutes late. Aiza often arrives early.

Examine

What does the information tell you?

- there are three children – Aiza, Frankie, Mo
- gym club starts at 4.30pm
- Aiza often arrives early
- gym club is on Wednesday
- Frankie can often be five minutes late

Interpret

What does the information not tell you?

- how early Aiza arrives
- when Mo arrives
- what they do at gym club
- if they like it

Deduce

Now using the information you have analysed, which sentence below must be true?

A Mo always arrives on time.

B Frankie sometimes arrives by 4.35pm.

C Aiza likes gymnastics.

Tip: Only choose a fact that is definitely shown in the information sentences.

Organising Information

A good way of sorting out all the information is to write it down in a table, list or chart. This makes it easier to understand and can help you work out the answer.

Let's start by reading the information in these sentences:

Dan, Rosie, Ahmed, Lena and Femi went on a woodland activity day.
- Everyone followed the trail.
- Dan, Rosie and Femi made some woodland crafts.
- Dan, Lena and Rosie built a den in the woods.

Who did the fewest activities?
Let's look at two ways to sort out the information provided in the sentences above.

We could use a tally chart.

Dan	III
Rosie	III
Ahmed	I
Lena	II
Femi	II

Or we could use a table.

Dan	Rosie	Ahmed	Lena	Femi
trail	trail	trail	trail	trail
craft	craft		den	craft
den	den			

If we look at our tables it's clear to see from both that Ahmed did the fewest activities.

Tip: Remember, the charts help you to make better sense of the information and quickly find the answer to a question.

GIVE IT A GO! Look at the different sorting methods we've explored together and decide which method works best for you.

Sort the information below to discover who joined the **fewest** clubs: Thea, Stefan, Jian or Meena?

Thea, Stefan, Jian and Meena have joined school clubs.
- Jian joined the science club.
- Everyone except Meena joined the football club.
- Stefan and Thea joined the art club.
- Meena joined the drama club.

Let's look at the question types in more detail.

Comprehension skills: examining, interpreting, deduction, organising

Comprehension: True or Untrue?

This **Reading Comprehension** question type asks you to use the information that you are given, and to decide which statement must be true or untrue about the subject covered in the information sentences.

Let's work through the question below together.
This question looks at the spelling test scores for five children.

Read the information, then work out the answer to the question.

Choose the correct answer.

Ana, Ella, Milo, Dylan and Scarlet have a spelling test.

There are ten spelling questions. There is a maximum of ten marks.

sentences explaining what the information is about

Ana and Milo got the same mark.

Dylan got four spellings wrong.

Ella got all the odd numbered questions correct.

Scarlet got half of Ana's mark.

information about how children performed in the spelling test

Only one of these sentences below is **true**. Which one?

A Milo got eight marks out of ten.

B Scarlet left out three spellings.

C Ella got a lower mark than Dylan.

D Ana had the lowest mark.

E Dylan got more than Milo.

answer options

Tip: Underline definite information in the sentences.

Examine

- The first two sentences tell us there are five children. There are ten spelling questions.
- Let's read through the information to find what we know.
  - The fourth line of information tells us that Dylan got four spellings wrong: this means he got six marks.
  - The fifth line tells us that Ella got odd numbered questions (1, 3, 5, 7, 9) correct: she got five marks.
  - The other sentences do not give us exact information about Ana's, Milo's and Scarlet's marks.

Interpret and sort information

- Let's interpret each answer sentence to find which one is true.
  - A Milo may have got eight marks, but he may have also got a lower mark. The sentence is **untrue**.
  - B We know Scarlet got half of Ana's mark, but we don't know if she left out three spellings. The sentence is **untrue**.
  - C We know Ella got five marks and Dylan got six marks. This sentence is **true**.
  - D Scarlet got a lower mark than Ana, so Ana couldn't have got the lowest mark. The sentence is **untrue**.
  - E We know Dylan got six marks, but we don't know Milo's exact mark. The sentence is **untrue**.

What is the answer?

Ella got a lower mark than Dylan.

LET'S PRACTISE!

Read the information, then work out the answers to the questions.

Find the correct answers and mark them in the boxes on the right.

1 Ezra, Becky and Reggie have to catch the school bus at 8.20am.

Reggie always catches the bus on time.

On Friday, Becky was late and missed the bus.

Only one of the sentences below is **true**. **Which one?**

A Ezra missed the school bus on Friday.

B Becky always gets to the bus stop before 8.20am.

C Reggie was late for school on Friday.

D Becky sometimes misses the school bus.

E Ezra gets to the bus stop before Reggie.

A B C D E

2 Chloe, Mila and Leo go to a cafe to buy ice creams.

The shop has lots of different flavours.

Leo likes vanilla ice cream, but Chloe prefers chocolate ice cream and strawberry ice cream.

Only one of the sentences below is **true**. **Which one?**

A Chloe buys a chocolate ice cream.

B Mila does not like ice cream.

C Leo likes vanilla ice cream.

D Leo and Mila like mint ice cream.

E The cafe only has three flavoured ice creams.

A B C D E

3 Sushma and Eva go along to a summer holiday activity club.

There is rollerblading, tennis and street dancing.

Sushma likes rollerblading best, but Eva prefers tennis and street dancing.

Only one of the sentences below is **not true**. **Which one?**

A Eva likes to go rollerblading least.

B There are three activities.

C Sushma prefers to go rollerblading.

D Eva likes street dancing.

E Sushma likes tennis the most.

A B C D E

Comprehension skills:
examining, interpreting, deduction, organising

Comprehension: Most or Fewest?

This **Reading Comprehension** question type asks you to use information to find the most or the fewest activities, items, people or measures.

Let's look at a question together.
In this question, you sort out the information from each sentence to find the answer.

Read the information below, then work out the answer to the question.
Choose the correct answer.

Class 4 is comparing heights of five model towers. — *sentence explaining what the information is about*

Tower 1 and Tower 3 are both 1 metre high.

Tower 4 is smaller than Tower 1, but taller than Tower 2.

Tower 5 is taller than Tower 3.

— *the information*

Which is the tallest tower?

A Tower 1 B Tower 2 C Tower 3 D Tower 4 E Tower 5 — *answer options*

- Let's start by reading the first line to find out what the information is about: heights of towers.
- Now, read the question to see what you need to find: the tallest tower.
- For practice papers, you can underline information or draw tables or lists to help you sort information. Aim to be able to sort out information without these by the time you do a real test.

Examine and interpret

- Underline two sentences that give definite information about the towers: lines 1 and 3 of the information text.
- The second line of information text gives two pieces of information about Tower 4.
  - It is smaller than Tower 1 (which means it is also smaller than Towers 3 and 5).
  - It is taller than Tower 2 (making Tower 2 the smallest tower).

Sort information

- There is a lot of information, so let's make a list or drawing to help sort it out.

  Here we have a five tower shapes to help visualise the different heights.

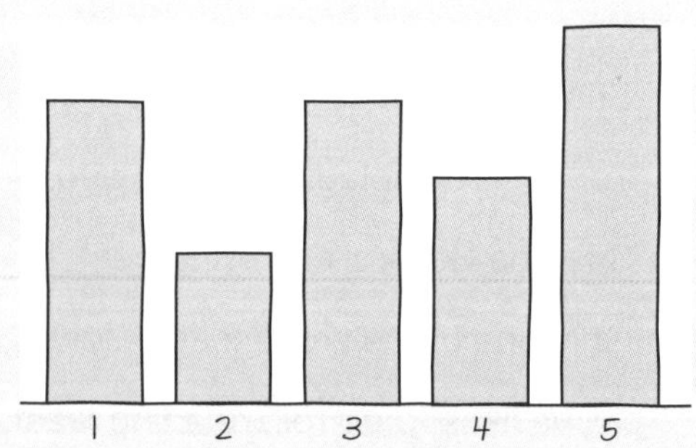

  Here we have made a list to show the height order of the five towers.

tallest ↑	5
	1 and 3
	4
smallest	2

  What is the answer?

Tower 5 is the **tallest** tower.

LET'S PRACTISE!

Read the information, then work out the answers to the questions.

Find the correct answers and mark them in the boxes on the right.

1 Min, Alex, Eleni, Dan and Lola are at the beach.

Eleni, Dan and Lola build a sandcastle.

Lola and Min swim in the sea.

Eleni flies her new kite.

Alex, Dan and Min play frisbee.

Min and Alex collect different shells.

Who does the most beach activities?

A Min B Alex C Eleni D Dan E Lola

A ☐ B ☐ C ☐ D ☐ E ☐

2 Last week, the weather in the UK turned cold.

On Monday and Wednesday, it was 3°C.

Friday was hotter than Wednesday but cooler than Tuesday.

Thursday was colder than Monday.

Which was the coldest day of the week?

A Monday B Tuesday C Wednesday D Thursday E Friday

A ☐ B ☐ C ☐ D ☐ E ☐

3 Beth, Pavel, Yasmeen, Jonas and Holly pack for a school weekend trip.

Beth, Pavel and Holly each have a suitcase.

Beth has a green satchel.

Jonas uses his backpack and a beach bag.

Pavel also uses a backpack.

Yasmeen and Holly both have a duffel bag.

Who has the fewest pieces of luggage?

A Beth B Pavel C Yasmeen D Jonas E Holly

A ☐ B ☐ C ☐ D ☐ E ☐

Making Words

There are seven **Making Words** question types. They test your skills in finding or making words by recognising letter and spelling patterns, spotting words within words, finding and following letter sequences, and using logic and finding clues.

Aa Word Study

Recognising Letter Spelling Patterns

Our words are a mix of letters and spelling patterns. Recognising letters, their patterns and positions in words can help us find or make new words in most of the **Making Words** question types.

Use this chart to revise the different spelling patterns.

Vowels	Almost all words contain one or more vowels: a, e, i, o, u. They can be in different positions in a word – at the beginning, middle or end.
Consonant groups	Two consonant letters making one sound, such as th, ch, sh, ph, wh, ck, ff, pp, bb, ss, zz. They can be in different positions in a word. Groups of two or three consonants where each sound is pronoounced.
Vowel groups	Two letters making one vowel sound, such as ai, ay, ee, ea, ie, oo, ow, oi, ou, aw. Three letters making one sound, such as air, ear, igh, tch, ure.
Consonant blends	Groups of two or three consonants where each sound is pronounced. Initial consonant blends, such as bl, cl, cr, dr, gl, pr, sk, st, scr, spl, thr. Final consonant blends, such as nt, ng, ft, lf, st, mp, sk, ld, lt.
Silent letters	Letters that cannot be heard, such as k – knot, w – write, h – whale, b – comb.
Spelling patterns examples	Prefixes (un, dis, re, etc) and suffixes (ness, less, ful, etc), words ending in 'y', compound words, past tense verb endings (ed, en).

Spotting Words Within Words

Most words can contain smaller words within them, eg 'eat', 'at' and 'ate' are in the word 'create'. More words can be made by taking out letters or putting them in a different order.

Finding or making smaller words within words is useful for question types **Make a Word**, **Hidden Words**, **Complete the Word**, **Move a Letter** and **Missing Words**.

GIVE IT A GO! Copy the table and add as many words as you can into it.

Find new words made by some of the letters in the word 'create'.

create		
three-letter words	**four-letter words**	**five-letter words**
ace	acre	crate
era	tear	

Finding and Following Letter Patterns

Using the word 'create', you've been able to find and rearrange its letters to make other words. These skills are used in the **Make a Word** and **Complete a Word** questions, which also focus on your ability to:

a. find a set pattern of letters
b. follow that exact pattern to create a new word.

Let's look at some letter patterns:

h**ay** **l**id = lay

The pattern is: 1st letter of second word and 2nd and 3rd letter of first word.

Let's follow the letter pattern using the two words below.

bag wet = ?

b**ag** **w**et

What is the new word?

Logic and Reasoning Skills

When you first look at **Making Words** questions, they can look tricky and confusing.

Don't panic! The tests encourage you to use your spelling and word skills, but they also want you to use your thinking skills to find and make new words. Here are a few tips:

- Work on what you know first and then work backwards.
- Once you have worked out one question you should find the rest easier to work out.

- Say the words with each possible answer.
- Listen to the word or letter that makes sense.

- Write out each possible answer to help you find the correct word or pattern.

- Remember to read the instruction sentences slowly.
- Look carefully at the example.

Let's look at the question types in more detail.

Make a Word

Word skills: finding and using letter patterns, logic and reasoning skills

Make a Word questions ask you to find the letter pattern used between the two words to make a new word. You can then use the same letter pattern to find the missing new word.

Let's look at two questions in detail.
In this question, the possible new word is four letters long.

The **three** words in the second set go together in **the same way** as the three words in the first set. Find the missing word in the second set.

Choose the correct answer.

(laid [dish] rush) (step [?] rock)

A pore B sock C peck D pest E spot

set 1

set 2

this is the word you are trying to find

Let's look at the first set of words:

- Some of the letters in 'laid' and 'rush' make the word 'dish'. What letter pattern is used?

  Write a number for each letter of 'laid' and 'rush':

1	2	3	4	5	6	7	8
l	a	i	d	r	u	s	h

The pattern is:

4	3	7	8
d	i	s	h

Let's use the letter pattern on the two words in the second set: 'step' and 'rock':

- Number pattern:

1	2	3	4	5	6	7	8
s	t	e	p	r	o	c	k

The pattern is:

4	3	7	8
p	e	c	k

Let's do one more. Try to work it out for yourself.

(grace [card] round) (blown [?] rinse)

A wore B snow C lose D none E worn

The answer is: A (wore). (b**low**n [wore] **r**inse)

How did you work it out?

- There are two 'r's in the first set of words that could be used to make the word 'card'.
- But in the second set, the pattern would have given us either 'wole' or 'wore'.
- The word 'wole' is not a real word or given in the answer choices.

LET'S PRACTISE!

In questions 1–7, the **three** words in the second set go together in **the same way** as the three words in the first set.

Find the missing word in the second set. Mark the correct answer in the box on the right.

1 (fox [for] red) (was [?] get)

A wag B saw C wet D set E age

2 (beg [got] dot) (pat [?] den)

A ate B tap C pad D ten E end

3 (float [take] biker) (lemon [?] water)

A late B note C moat D leer E mate

4 (ready [reach] chimp) (clamp [?] shrug)

A cramp B crash C lurch D slump E clash

5 (prose [star] thank) (spice [?] leans)

A nice B plan C clap D seep E pile

6 (pawn [pain] rail) (boat [?] tear)

A rota B bear C rate D beat E bare

7 (sour [bus] best) (trim [?] frog)

A fir B tog C fit D rim E rot

Complete the Word

Word skills: finding and using letter patterns, letter/spelling patterns, words within words

Complete the Word questions ask you to follow the letter pattern used by two pairs of words. The second word could be a smaller word within the first word. It might also be made from a mix of letters similar to the patterns in **Make a Word** questions.

Let's examine some questions together.
In this question, there is a simple letter pattern.

The question below has three pairs of words.

Find the word that finishes the last pair of words in **the same way** as the first two pairs of words.

Choose the correct answer.

(long log) (tray try) (seat [?])

A sat B sea C ate D set E tea

this is the word you are trying to find

look at these pairs of words to find the pattern

- Let's look at the first pair of words. The letter 'n' is not used in the second word.
- The second word is made up of the first, second and fourth letters of the first word: l, o, g.
- The second pair of words follow the same pattern. The first, second and fourth letters make the word 'try'.
- Now we can use the pattern to find the missing second word in the last pair.

The answer is the word **set**.

Yes! ✔

The 1st, 2nd and 4th letters make 'set' (**se**a**t**).

Here's another question. Can you work out the missing word for yourself?

(stick kit) (crane ear) (stamp [?])

A map B pat C sat D sam E sap

Tip: Number the letters in the first words to help see the pattern (see **Make a Word** on page 28).

The answer is: B (pat).

How did you work it out?

- In the first pair, the first word letter pattern makes the word 'kit': s**t**i**c**k.
- In the second pair, the same letter pattern makes the word 'ear': c**ra**n**e**.

If you number the letters in the first words you'll see that the second word of each pair is made up of letters 5, 3 and 2 of the first word:

s	t	i	c	k	k	i	t	c	r	a	n	e	e	a	r
1	2	3	4	5	5	3	2	1	2	3	4	5	5	3	2

- That means that the second word in the third pair is 'pat': s**ta**m**p**.

LET'S PRACTISE!

Questions 1–7 have three pairs of words.

Find the words that finishes the last pair of words in **the same way** as the first two pairs of words.

Mark the correct answer in the box on the right.

1 (tent ten) (herb her) (pear [?])

A tap B ear C ape D pea E era

2 (plain plan) (feast feat) (coast [?])

A cost B oats C coat D cots E cats

3 (carry cry) (taken ten) (below [?])

A lob B low C web D bow E owl

4 (birth rib) (tense net) (trade [?])

A red B rat C tar D are E art

5 (rusted dust) (singer ring) (basket [?])

A bake B east C task D take E base

6 (catching hang) (forecast cost) (sunblock [?])

A luck B sunk C club D lock E buns

7 (sword sow) (place pal) (frown [?])

A now B own C for D won E row

Insert a Letter

Word skills: word types, letter/spelling patterns, spelling strategies, logic skills

Insert a Letter questions ask you to find one letter, from a selection of five letters, that is able to complete four words. The letter is at the end and beginning of the words. The words are a mix of word types such as nouns, verbs, adjectives, pronouns and adverbs.

Let's take a look and see what the questions are all about.
In this question, you need to make two three-letter words and two four-letter words.

The **same** letter must go into **both** sets of brackets.

The letter ends the word in front of the brackets and begins the word after the brackets.

Choose the correct answer.

ca [?] ug fee [?] all — *the missing letters*

A j B b C d D t E n — *five letter choices*

Let's look at the first set of letters: ca [?] ug:
- Add each of the five letters onto the end of 'ca' to make it into a word.
- Say each word out loud or write them down: ca**j** ✗ ca**b** ✓ ca**d** ✓ ca**t** ✓ ca**n** ✓
- Do the same to the beginning of 'ug': **j**ug ✓ **b**ug ✓ **d**ug ✓ **t**ug ✓ **n**ug ✗
- The only letters that can make both words are: **b**, **d** and **t**.

Now let's look at the second set of letters: fee [?] all:
- We only have three letters left. Try them at the end and beginning of the second set of letters:
  fee**b** ✗ fee**d** ✓ fee**t** ✓ **b**all ✓ **d**all ✗ **t**all ✓

It is the only letter that can make all four words:
ca**t** ✓ **t**ug ✓ fee**t** ✓ **t**all ✓

Let's do another one. Try to work it out for yourself.

Tip: Say and sound out each set of letters before and after the bracket.

thum [?] ath shru [?] asic

A p B r C g D m E b

The answer is: E (the letter b).

How did you do it?
- In the first set: thum**p** ✓ thum**r** ✗ thum**g** ✗ thum**m** ✗ thum**b** ✓
  path ✓ **r**ath ✗ **g**ath ✗ **m**ath ✓ **b**ath ✓
- Only the letters **p** and **b** can make both words.
- In the second set: shru**p** ✗ shru**b** ✓ **p**asic ✗ **b**asic ✓

LET'S PRACTISE!

In questions 1–7, the **same** letter must go into **both** sets of brackets.

The letter ends the word in front of the brackets and begins the word after the brackets.

Mark the correct answer in the box on the right.

1 duc [?] ing pin [?] ind

A g B r C k D f E t

2 sho [?] ait cla [?] ent

A w B t C p D b E d

3 tow [?] ight plai [?] ews

A m B s C t D p E n

4 sig [?] ung dis [?] and

A s B n C h D k E b

5 an [?] ard wa [?] our

A t B y C s D c E g

6 wor [?] ream ban [?] ig

A c B m C g D k E d

7 shar [?] it slee [?] air

A p B t C k D n E h

Move a Letter

Word skills: word types, word structure, words within words, letter/ spelling patterns

Move a Letter questions ask you to make two new words by moving a letter from the first word to the second word. It encourages you to look for words within words and spelling patterns.

Let's get to grips with the questions by looking at some in detail.

Make **two** new words by moving one letter from the first word to the second word.

Do not rearrange the letters in any other way and **both** the new words need to make sense.

Choose the correct answer.

trail for

A t B r C a D i E l

a letter moves from this word

a letter moves to this word

Let's look at the first five-letter word: 'trail':

- Move one letter to change it into a four-letter word.
- What four-letter words can you see?
- Move 't' and the new word is 'rail'. Move 'r' and the new word is 'tail'.
- This means that we could use 't' or 'r' to make a new second word.

Let's look at the second word: 'for':

- Look at the spelling pattern of the word. Where could 't' be placed?
- Say or write down the word that also includes the letter 't'.
- Do the same with the letter 'r'.
- Only 't' turns 'for' into a new word.

Tip: For the second word, write down possible places where the new letter might go.

Move **t** from **train**. Add it to the end of **for**. The new words are **rail** and **fort**.

Let's have a go at another one. Try to work it out for yourself.

Tip: The words can change into a different word type, eg noun to verb.

wheat step

A w B h C e D a E t

The answer is: C (the letter e).

How did you do it?

- Take 'e' from the first word.
- Move 'e' to the second word and add it to the middle to be 'ee'.
- If we try moving any of the other letters from the first word to the second we discover that we can't make a new word.

LET'S PRACTISE!

In questions 1–7, make **two** new words by moving one letter from the first letter to the second word.

Do not rearrange the letters in any other way and **both** the new words need to make sense.

Mark the correct answer in the box on the right.

1 rocky ours

A r B o C c D k E y

A B C D E

2 along sty

A a B l C o D n E g

A B C D E

3 feast and

A f B e C a D s E t

A B C D E

4 thing bean

A t B h C i D n E g

A B C D F

5 drown late

A d B r C o D w E n

A B C D E

6 lance limb

A l B a C n D c E e

A B C D E

7 break hose

A b B r C e D a E k

A B C D E

Word skills: word types, word structure, letter/ spelling patterns

Hidden Words

Hidden Words questions ask you to find a four-letter word hidden within a sentence. The letters of the hidden word are between the end of one word and the start of another. The questions also test your skills in recognising letter and spelling patterns within words.

We can see how the questions work by looking at some examples.

A **four-letter word** is hidden at the **end** of one word and the **start** of the next word.

Find the two words that contain the hidden word.

Choose the correct answer.

The cliffs are steep to climb.

The cliffs	cliffs are	are steep	steep to	to climb.
A	B	C	D	E

the sentence

options for where the four-letter word could be hidden in the words of the sentence above

- Let's read the sentence first: The cliffs are steep to climb.
- The sentence is split into five two-word answer sections, eg The cliffs, cliffs are, etc.
- Focus on one section at a time.
- Remember, the letters of the hidden word are **between** the two words (see tip box).
- Let's look at section A: 'The cliffs'.
  - Can you see any spelling patterns that can be part of a word?
  - Check or write down possible four-word formations to see if they make sense. eg the cliffs the cliffs the cliffs, etc.
- Do this with each of the five sections in the answer options.

Tip: The hidden word has to have at least one letter in both words.

The answer is **C**.

Yes!

The hidden word is 'rest' – a**re st**eep.

A clue was the final consonant blend 'st' and the vowel 'e' before it!

Let's practise another one. Can you work this one out for yourself?

Mia bought a comb and brush.

Mia bought	bought a	a comb	comb and	and brush.
A	B	C	D	E

The answer is: D (com**b and**).

How did you do it?

- The hidden word is between the two words 'comb and'.
- The second word is 'and'.
- The end of the first word has a consonant, 'b'.

Together they make the word **band**.

LET'S PRACTISE!

In sentences 1–7, a **four-letter word** is hidden at the **end** of one word and the **start** of the next word.

Find the two words that contain the hidden word.

Mark the correct answer in the box on the right.

1 Please stop eating the birthday cake.

Please stop	stop eating	eating the	the birthday	birthday cake.
A	B	C	D	E

2 The scary dragon grabbed the unicorn.

The scary	scary dragon	dragon grabbed	grabbed the	the unicorn.
A	B	C	D	E

3 The cheeky princess often played tricks.

The cheeky	cheeky princess	princess often	often played	played tricks.
A	B	C	D	E

4 The cross king stamped his feet.

The cross	cross king	king stamped	stamped his	his feet.
A	B	C	D	E

5 Leo broke his elbow last night.

Leo broke	broke his	his elbow	elbow last	last night.
A	B	C	D	E

6 The hotel seems to be closed.

The hotel	hotel seems	seems to	to be	be closed.
A	B	C	D	E

7 The hungry fox was chasing rabbits.

The hungry	hungry fox	fox was	fox chasing	chasing rabbits.
A	B	C	D	E

Missing Words

Word skills: letter/spelling patterns, words within words, letter/spelling patterns, logic and reasoning skills

Missing Words questions ask you to choose three missing letters that complete a word within a sentence. The word is in capital letters.

Let's look at some questions in detail.

The word in capitals in the sentence below has had **three letters** taken out.

These letters can make one correctly spelled three-letter word. The sentence must make sense.

Choose the correct answer.

Tom ate a big juicy **CH**.

A BEA B TEA C MAT D PEA E ATE

this word is missing three letters

one of these options completes the word above

- Let's start by reading the sentence for clues about what the incomplete word could be.
  - Tom is eating something which is big and juicy. It has the letters CH in it.
  - Fruits can be juicy and '**ch**erry' and 'pea**ch**' both use CH.
- Now let's look at any spelling patterns for clues.
  - The CH could be a digraph. The three-letter answers would go before or after the CH.
  - The CH could be the first letter (C) and the last letter (H) with the three letters in the middle.
- Let's check all five three-letter answer words.
  - Say or write down the different possibilities:
    BEACH CHBEA CBEAH; TEACH, CHTEA, CTEAH; MATCH, CHMAT, CMATH; PEACH, CHPEA, CPEAH; CHATE, ATECH, CATEH
    Remember that the word must make sense within the sentence.

PEA + CH = PEACH

Tom ate a big juicy **peach**.

PEA is the only answer that can be used with CH and make sense in the sentence.

Tip: The capital letters are used to help you focus on the incomplete words and the possible answers.

Try to working this one out for yourself following the steps above.

I put on my football **SF** for the match.

A CAN B TAR C CAR D COT E EAR

The answer is: C (CAR).

How did you do it?

- The sentence subject gives clues that the word could be a scarf.
- None of the three-letter words can go before or after **SF** to make a real word.
- The only three-letter word that fits with **SF** is **CAR**.

LET'S PRACTISE!

In sentences 1–7, the words in capitals have had **three letters** taken out.

These letters can make one correctly spelled three-letter word. The sentence must make sense.

Mark the correct answer in the box on the right.

1 We love to eat **HY** on toast.

A ONE B ACE C ARE D ICE E ODE

2 King Midas put the golden **CR** on his head.

A ATE B OWN C END D OWE E EVE

3 The diver found a **PL** on the seabed.

A USE B AIR C EAR D AGE E RIM

4 A **GIGIC** eagle swooped across the lagoon.

A ACT B ANT C ROC D RAT E LET

5 The tailor made many expensive **GARTS**.

A MEN B MAN C END D TEN E ORE

6 Zoe and Ana **SH** a bedroom.

A OUT B ELF C APE D RUG E ARE

7 Rory is **TING** the string off his parcel.

A CUT B CAT C RIP D ROT E WIN

Word skills: letter patterns, words within words, logic and reasoning skills

Joining Words

Joining Words questions ask you to choose a word from each group to make one new word. Some of the words are compound word, eg raindrop. Others are words that together make a new word with a very different meaning, eg 'wag' + 'on' = wagon.

Let's examine some questions together.
This question contains a compound word.

Choose **one** word from each of the **two** groups to form **one** new word.

Do **not** change the letter order. The words from the first group must come first.

Choose **both** correct answers.

(ear eye red) (sniff hat lash)

A ear	X sniff
B eye	Y hat
C red	Z lash

first set of words

second set of words

choose one word from each column

- Read the first word in the first group: 'ear'.
- Read it or say it with each of the words in the second group: ear – sniff, ear – hat, ear – lash.
- Do any of the words make one word?
- Repeat the same action with the other two words – 'eye' and 'red' – in group one.

Yes!

The word **eyelash** is a compound word.

It names the lashes around the eyes.

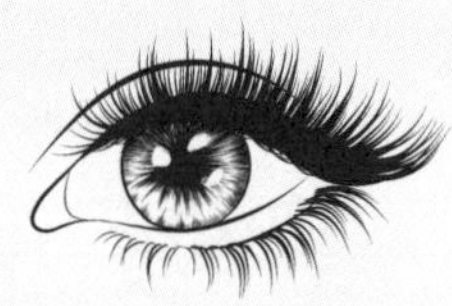

See if you can work out this question for yourself.

(up by do) (art set like)

A up	X art
B by	Y like
C do	Z set

Tip: Say the different words together a few times to hear the correct word, eg beg – in begin.

The answer is: AZ (upset).

How did you work it out?

- Match each word in the first group with the second group.
- The words 'up' and 'set' are the only words that can be joined together to make a new word: upset.

LET'S PRACTISE!

In questions 1–6, choose **one** word from each of the **two** groups to form **one** new word.

Do **not** change the letter order. The words from the first group must come first.

Mark **both** correct answers in the boxes on the right.

1 (one do rot) (son ten net)

A one X son
B do Y ten
C rot Z net

A B C X Y Z

2 (sail jump catch) (see in or)

A sail X see
B jump Y in
C catch Z or

A B C X Y Z

3 (snow rain thunder) (drip flake fog)

A snow X drip
B rain Y flake
C thunder Z fog

A B C X Y Z

4 (book spoon tale) (it let act)

A book X it
B spoon Y let
C tale Z act

A B C X Y Z

5 (spot lion neat) (less full side)

A spot X less
B lion Y full
C neat Z side

A B C X Y Z

6 (mix pan pot) (roll top cake)

A mix X roll
B pan Y top
C pot Z cake

A B C X Y Z

Codes

There are four **Codes** question types. They test your skills in recognising and using alphabetical order, finding a link between letters, finding and using different patterns, and logic and reasoning.
The four **Codes** question types all use letters in their codes. To find an answer for each code question, you need to find letter patterns that are linked to the alphabet or number patterns.

Code-breaking Strategies

Letter Code Patterns

In **Letter Series** and **Letter Connections** questions, look closely at the given codes or sequences for simple letter patterns.

Look at this simple code sequence. AD BD CE DE ?

The first letters in each pair are in alphabetical order starting from A: ABCD

The second letters in each pair are in a simple two-letter pattern: DDEE

The code pattern helps us find the next pair of letters: EF

Mirror Code Patterns

In **Letter Series**, **Letter Connections** and **Related Words**, there may be times when two letters from either end of the alphabet are paired together. This is when a mirror code pattern can be used.

It is a good idea to learn the mirror pairs off by heart, eg BY, where B is the second letter from the start of the alphabet and Y is the second letter from the end of the alphabet.

The mirror letter for F is U (they are both the 6th letters from each end).

1	2	3	4	5	6	7	8	9	10	11	12	13	13	12	11	10	9	8	7	6	5	4	3	2	1
A	B	C	D	E	F	G	H	I	J	K	L	M/	N	O	P	Q	R	S	T	U	V	W	X	Y	Z

Tip: Draw the alphabet on paper and number the letters from 1–13 to see mirror letter pairs.

Word Letter Patterns and Logic

The question type **Word Number Codes** uses skills in logic and letter patterns within words to work out which words are matched to which number code, eg

N	O	T	E
1	2	3	4

L	A	T	E
5	6	3	4

L	O	O	T
5	2	2	3

matching words and codes helps you to work out the codes for new words

by looking at the numbers corresponding to the letters in the words on the left we can work out that the code for LOOT is 5223

Counting Patterns

Some **Letter Series**, **Letter Connections** and **Related Words** questions encourage you to find a counting pattern (forwards or backwards) between the letters in the alphabet.

In verbal reasoning tests, the alphabet is one continuous circle. You can count forward from the end of the alphabet to the start of the alphabet or count backwards.

For example: **Y** (count 3 letters forward) = **B**   **L** (count 4 letters back) = **H**

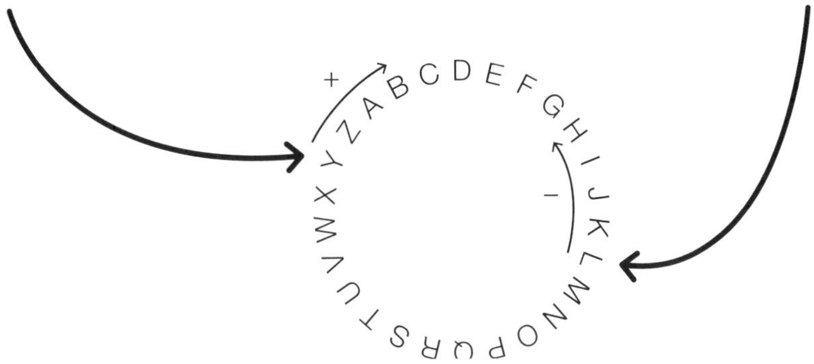

Tip: Write out the alphabet to help you count between the letters to find the pattern.

GIVE IT A GO! Crack and write codes with counting patterns.

The code for **BIRD** is **ZKPF**. The counting pattern is: **–2, +2, –2, +2**

B (2 letters back) = **Z**   **I** (2 letters forward) = **K**   **R** (2 letters back) = **P**   **D** (2 letters forward) = **F**

Use the counting pattern and alphabet above to write new codes for:

WORM	FISH	CAMEL

Tips for Code Breaking

Code questions can seem confusing and difficult, but using the suggestions and tips will make them easier to solve.

Let's look at the question types in more detail.

Letter Series

Word skills: alphabet skills, links between letters, counting patterns

Letter Series questions ask you to find the pattern between sets of pairs of letters and use them to find the next two letters in the series.

Let's look at some questions in more detail.
Use the alphabet below to help you with both questions below.

A B C D E F G H I J K L M N O P Q R S T U V W X Y Z

Find the next two letters in the series.

Choose the correct answer.

ZD AF BH CJ [?]

A DK **B** DL **C** BI **D** DH **E** CL

There are two ways to find the next two letters:

1 Alphabet pattern:
- Look at the first letter of each pair. They go forward along the alphabet: Z A B C
- Look at the second letter of each pair. They are alternate letters: D F H J

2 Counting pattern:
- Count the letters between the first letters in a pair and then the second letters.
- The first letters go +1 letter forward.
- The second letters go +2 letters forward.

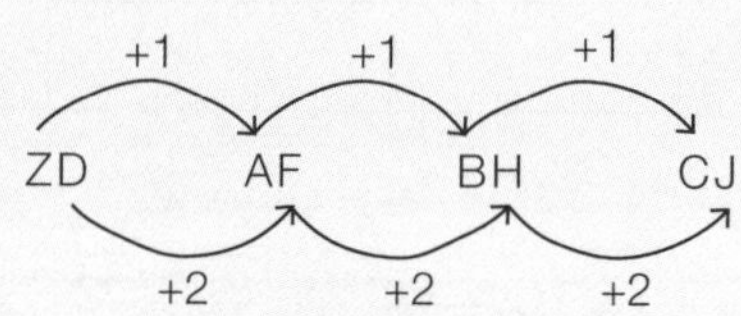

The next letter after C (+1) is **D**.

The second letter after J (+2) is **L**.

Tip: Jumping over letters to find a pattern is called leapfrogging.

Here's another question to try. Can you work it out for yourself?

MN OK QH SE [?]

A TB **B** UG **C** UB **D** QV **E** UD

Tip: To help you work it out while you're practising, write out the letters and your counting marks on a separate sheet of paper.

The answer is: C (UB).

How did you work it out?
- Count 2 letters forward for the 1st letters in pairs.
- Count 3 letters back for the 2nd letters in pairs.

LET'S PRACTISE!

In questions 1–7, find the next two letters in the series.

Use the alphabet below to help you.

Mark the correct answer in the box on the right.

A B C D E F G H I J K L M N O P Q R S T U V W X Y Z

1 AR BS CT DU [?]

A EF B EV C VW D EE E FW

2 XH UI RJ OK LL [?]

A JM B OM C IN D IM E MM

3 TU TS PQ PO LM [?]

A LK B PK C TK D LN E PM

4 YU XV WW VX UY [?]

A TX B VZ C AZ D TY E TZ

5 AD CC EB GA IZ [?]

A JY B KA C KY D LZ E HA

6 HW KT NQ QN TK [?]

A VH B WH C VL D WI E XH

7 EH JL OP TT [?]

A YY B XY C XX D YX E WX

Letter Connections

Word skills: alphabet skills, links between letters, counting patterns (+ and –), mirror patterns

Letter Connections questions ask you to complete the last part of a letter sentence by using a pair of letters that match the letter codes in the first part of the sentence.

Let's get to grips with this question type by looking at some together.
Use the alphabet below to help you with both questions below.

A B C D E F G H I J K L M N O P Q R S T U V W X Y Z

Find the letters that will help the sentence make sense.

Choose the correct answer.

LM is to **KP** as **RS** is to [?]

A QR B ST C QV D SP E QT

Start by looking at the first part of the sentence: LM is to KP.

- Look at the first letters of each pair. Think about where the letters sit in the alphabet: We count back one letter to get from L to K (–1).
- Now look at the second letters of each pair: We count forwards three letters to get from M to P (+3)

Use the same pattern to complete the second part of the sentence: RS is to ?

- The first letter is R. The pattern tells us to count back one letter: R (–1) = Q
- The second letter is S. The pattern tells us to count forwards three letters: S (+3) = V

The missing letters must match RS using the same pattern as the first two pairs.

LM is to **KP** as **RS** is to **QV**.

Here's another one to try.
In this question, there is no counting pattern. It uses mirror pairs instead.

Tip: Go back to page 42 to find out more about mirror codes.

ZS is to **AH** as **XY** is to [?]

A WV B CB C AB D BC E DF

The answer is: B (CB).

How did you work it out?

- If there is a mirror pair in the sentence, it is likely to be a mirror code.
- Use the alphabet to check to see if ZS and AH are mirror pairs.
- This means that the missing pair of letters are the mirror letters of XY.

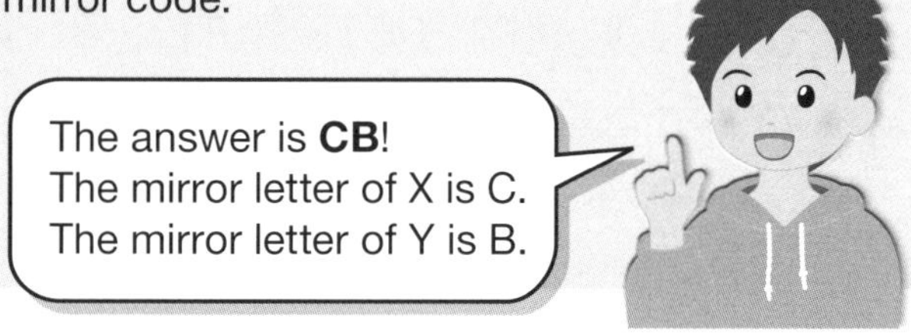

LET'S PRACTISE!

Find the letters that will help the sentences in questions 1–7 make sense.

Use the alphabet below to help you.

Mark the correct answer in the box on the right.

A B C D E F G H I J K L M N O P Q R S T U V W X Y Z

1 **AB** is to **CD** as **MN** is to [?]

A OQ B KL C OP D PQ E NO

2 **BC** is to **DE** as **QR** is to [?]

A ST B RS C TS D PQ E FG

3 **EF** is to **HI** as **TU** is to [?]

A VW B RS C UV D US E WX

4 **IL** is to **GM** as **NQ** is to [?]

A JP B QT C LO D LR E PR

5 **NO** is to **KP** as **WX** is to [?]

A YT B SY C TY D TX E UZ

6 **XC** is to **ZA** as **RI** is to [?]

A PK B TG C TH D TF E SO

7 **AB** is to **ZY** as **CD** is to [?]

A XW B XY C UV D EF E ZY

Related Words

Word skills: links between letters, counting patterns (+ and –), mirror patterns, codes to words/words to codes

Related Words questions ask you to work out the code of the word using its letter pattern. You then use the same letter pattern to find the code of a given word or find the word of a given code.

We can see how these questions work by looking at some in detail.
Use the alphabet below to help you with both questions.

A B C D E F G H I J K L M N O P Q R S T U V W X Y Z

In this question, we need to find the code for the word EMU.

Work out the **different** code for **each** of these questions.

Choose the correct answer.

If the code for **PEG** is **RGI**, what is the code for **EMU**?

A CKS　　B GOW　　C FNV　　D DLT　　E FOW

- On a piece of paper, write the word above the code.

P E G
↓
R G I

- Look for a pattern between the first letter of PEG (P) and the first letter of the code RGI (R).
- We can count two letters forward (+2) to get from P to R.
- If we look at the second and third letters in the word PEG and code RGI, we see that we can count two letters forward (+2) between these letters too E (+2) = G and G (+2) = I.

We can now use the (+2) counting pattern to find the code for **EMU**.

E (+2) = G　　**M** (+2) = O　　**U** (+2) = W

Let's try another question.
In this question, we need to work out the word from the code VLMG.

If the code for **KITE** is **JLSH** what does **VLMG** mean?

A MIND　　B SEND　　C WALK　　D WIND　　E RAIN

Tip: Remember to write the code above the word if you need to find the word.

The answer is: C (WALK).

How did you work it out?

- This time write the code above the word.

J L S H
↓
K I T E

- The counting pattern is: J to K (+1), L to I (–3), S to T (+1), H to E (–3)
- Use this counting pattern to work out the word for VLMG.
  V (+1) = W　　L (–3) = I　　M (+1) = N　　G (–3) = D

LET'S PRACTISE!

Work out the **different** code for **each** of these questions.

Use the alphabet below to help you.

Mark the correct answer in the box on the right.

A B C D E F G H I J K L M N O P Q R S T U V W X Y Z

1 If the code for **ANT** is **BOU**, what is the code for **CAR**?

A ADS B DBS C DBR D EPT E BZQ

2 If the code for **TOAD** is **VQCF**, what does **NGCR** mean?

A REAP B LEAK C JUMP D LEAP E NEWT

3 If the code for **KNIFE** is **IPGHC**, what is the code for **BREAD**?

A ZTCCB B DPGYF C ZRCBD D AQDZC E CSFBE

4 If the code for **JUMP** is **KWNR**, what is the code for **CLIMB**?

A BJHKA B DJJKE C DNJOC D DNJPB E DMKOC

5 If the code for **HER** is **DBP**, what does **FXK** mean?

A JAR B PAM C JUG D KIT E JAM

6 If the code for **POND** is **QRSK**, what is the code for **LAKE**?

A MCOL B MDPL C KXFX D NEQM E MDQR

7 If the code for **GREEN** is **JOHBQ**, what does **EORTQ** mean?

A BEACH B TREES C MAUVE D BROWN E BLACK

Word skills: logic skills, letter patterns in words

Word Number Codes

Word Number Code questions give you four words and three number codes. Each number represents a letter used in the words. The questions ask you to match the number codes to the correct words. You can then use the numbers to solve other codes.

There are two parts to this type of question.
In the first part, we need to match the correct number code to a word.

Tip: Start by looking at the letters which are in more than one word.

Three of the four words are given in code.

One of the codes is missing. The number codes are **not** in the same order as the words.

Choose the correct answer.

LANE FLEA LIFE NAIL — four words

1526 2163 1346 — three codes

- There are six letters used in the four words above: **A E F I L N**.
- Start by looking at the words and the codes. What patterns can you see? LANE and LIFE start with an L and end with an E. Can we see that pattern in the numbers? 1526 and 1346 both start and end with 1 and 6. So this must mean that 1 = L and 6 = E.
- Now we know the numbers for L and E, we can add them to all the words.

L	A	N	E	F	L	E	A	L	I	F	E	N	A	I	L
1			6		1	6		1			6				1

- Look at the number codes again. FLEA is the only word that matches the number code, 2<u>16</u>3. This means that F = 2 and A = 3. Let's add the numbers under the letters.

L	A	N	E	F	L	E	A	L	I	F	E	N	A	I	L
1	3		6	2	1	6	3	1		2	6		3		1

- We can now easily match the last two number codes to the words
  LIFE is 1526 FLEA is 2163 LANE is 1346 NAIL is 4351
- Write out the code numbers: 1 = L 2 = F 3 = A 4 = N 5 = I 6 = E
- We can see that the missing code is for NAIL (4351).

Now we know the numbers for each letter we can answer the question below.

Find the word for the number code **2351**.

A NAIL **B** FEEL **C** FAIL **D** LINE **E** LEAF

2	3	5	1
F	**A**	**I**	**L**

LET'S PRACTISE!

For questions 1–6, three of the four words are given in code.

One of the codes is missing. The number codes are **not** in the same order as the words.

Mark the correct answer in the box on the right.

SPOT	POLE	PEST	LOSE
5342	6531	4362	

1 Find the code for the word **PEST**.

A 5361 B 5261 C 1261 D 5216 E 1326

A B C D E

2 Find the word with the number code **4266**.

A TELL B SETT C LESS D TOLL E SELL

A B C D E

3 Find the code for the word **SLOT**.

A 6532 B 6125 C 5316 D 3516 E 6431

A B C D E

4 Find the word with the number code **6342**.

A SOLE B ELSE C STOP D ETTA E OLAF

A B C D E

5 Find the word for the number code **1334**.

A POOL B TOOL C SOOT D LOOP E PEEP

A B C D E

6 Find the code for the word **SOLO**.

A 3643 B 2462 C 5343 D 6343 E 6342

A B C D E

Maths Skills

There are four **Maths Skills** question types. They test your skills in the four operations and their rules, finding links between numbers, finding and using number patterns, and logic and problem solving.

Number Skills

Four Number Operations

All four **Maths Skills** question types encourage you to use your knowledge in addition, subtraction, multiplication and division to help find the answers.

Before attempting the **Maths Skills** questions, it is a good idea to revise these four number operations:

Number operation	Example
Addition (+)	Adding two or more numbers. 35 + 24 = 59
Subtraction (–)	Subtract one number from another (usually the biggest number). 25 – 15 = 10
Multiplication (×)	Repeated addition of a number. Three plates with four cakes on each. How many cakes in total? 3 × 4 = 12 cakes
Division (÷)	Sharing or grouping a number into smaller equal groups. Divide 15 cakes onto 3 plates. 15 ÷ 3 = 5

Tip: It is useful to know your times tables for multiplication and division questions.

Number Patterns

Number Series and **Related Numbers** question types encourage you to use numbers and the four operations to find patterns and solve puzzles.

GIVE IT A GO! Solve this number pyramid puzzle using an addition pattern.

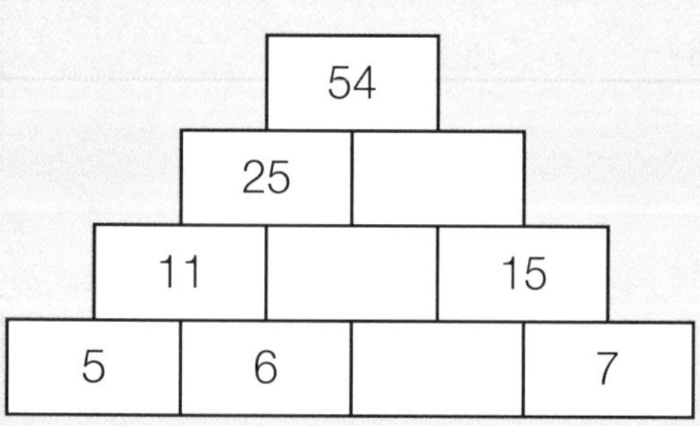

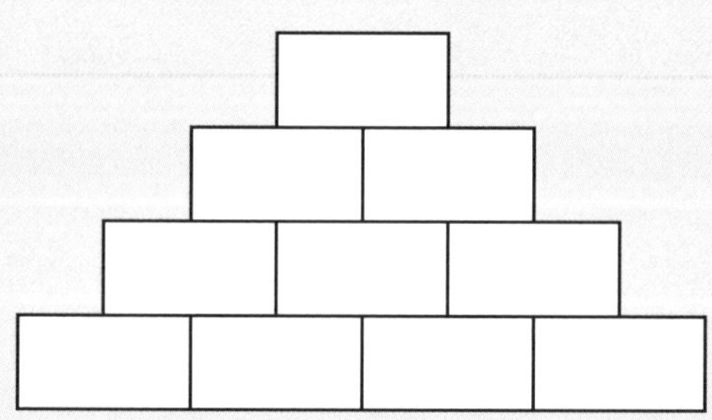

Create your own number pyramid puzzle for a friend. Use a subtraction pattern.

Number Patterns and Links

Number Series questions test skills in finding and using a range of patterns, including:

- counting patterns going forwards and backwards
- addition and subtraction patterns
- multiplication patterns

Tip: The leapfrog method is a good way to find and record a pattern.

Number Calculations

Complete the Calculation and **Letters for Numbers** questions focus on long calculations using a mix of the four operations. It is important to remember this rule to find the correct total:

Always start with division and multiplication from left to right and continue with addition and subtraction.

Here's an example: $18 + 3 \times 3 = ?$ $18 + (3 \times 3)$ $18 + 9 = 27$

Check Your Answer

There are a couple of ways you can check your answer if you are unsure of it.

1 Use an inverse operation to see if the numbers work together correctly. You can do this for addition and subtraction operations or multiplication and division operations.

For example:

- Addition: $23 + 17 = 40$ or Subtraction check: $40 - 17 = 23$
- Multiplication: $6 \times 3 = 18$ or Division check: $18 \div 6 = 3$

2 Check the five given answers and eliminate the answers you know are definitely wrong. Use logic before selecting your final answer.

Tips for Solving the Maths Skills Questions

Maths questions can seem confusing and difficult, but using these tips will make them easier to solve.

Let's look at the question types in more detail.

Complete the Calculation

Word skills: number patterns, addition, subtraction, division, multiplication

Complete the Calculation questions ask you to work out the first part of a calculation and then choose the missing number in the second part so that the answer for both parts is the same.

Let's look at some questions in detail.
In the first question, we need to use our knowledge of multiplication, addition and subtraction.

Find the number that finishes the calculation.

Choose the correct answer.

$2 \times 9 + 10 = 32 + 4 - [\ ?\ ]$

A 4 B 5 C 6 D 8 E 10

first calculation

second calculation

answer options for missing number

Start by working out the first calculation to find the answer:

- We multiply 2×9 which is 18.
- Then we add 10 to 18: $18 + 10 = 28$.
- The answer to the first calculation is 28.

Now work out the second calculation:

- We add 4 to 32: $32 + 4 = 36$.
- Now we need to choose a number that will also give the answer of 28.
- Let's do the maths! $36 - (\ ?\ ) = 28$
- The correct number is one of the five number answers.

Tip: If you are unsure of the correct answer, try the calculation with each of the five answer options to see which one works.

$2 \times 9 + 10 = 28$ $32 + 4 - \mathbf{8} = 28$

$2 \times 9 + 10 = 32 + 4 - \mathbf{8}$

Let's do one more. Work it out for yourself.

$30 \div 5 + 9 = 11 \times 2 - [\ ?\ ]$

A 5 B 6 C 7 D 9 E 10

The answer is: C (7).

How did you work it out?

- The first calculation is: $30 \div 5 = 6$ $6 + 9 = 15$
- The second calculation is: $11 \times 2 = 22$ $22 - 7 = 15$

LET'S PRACTISE!

In questions 1–7, find the number that finishes the calculations.

Mark the correct answer in the box on the right.

1 $5 + 7 = 9 + [\ ?\ ]$

A 1 B 2 C 3 D 4 E 5

2 $29 - 7 = 5 \times 2 + [\ ?\ ]$

A 9 B 10 C 11 D 12 E 14

3 $4 \times 10 = 5 \times [\ ?\ ]$

A 4 B 8 C 9 D 11 E 12

4 $33 \div 3 = 8 + 9 - [\ ?\ ]$

A 1 B 3 C 6 D 4 E 5

5 $25 \div 5 \times 3 + 5 = 26 - [\ ?\ ]$

A 1 B 2 C 3 D 5 E 6

6 $5 \times 9 - 10 + 1 = 48 + 2 - [\ ?\ ]$

A 10 B 12 C 13 D 14 E 16

7 $6 + 5 \times 2 + 4 = 12 \times [\ ?\ ] - 4$

A 2 B 4 C 6 D 8 E 10

Number Series

Word skills: number connections/ patterns, leapfrog counting, addition, subtraction, multiplication, logic and reasoning

Number Series questions ask you to find the pattern between a set of numbers in a series or sequence and use it to choose the last missing number. The patterns can include addition, subtraction, multiplication and division of numbers. Some numbers may go forwards and others go backwards within one sequence.

Let's examine some questions together.
In this question, look for a pattern between alternate numbers.

Find the number that continues the series in the best way.

Choose the correct answer.

5 12 6 13 7 14 [?] — missing number in the series

A 15 B 13 C 8 D 7 E 10 — options for missing number

Start by looking for any clear pattern in the series (sequence).

- In this example, there is a straightforward pattern between alternate numbers.
- Use the leapfrog method to jump over numbers to check the pattern.

5 12 6 13 7 14 ?

- The first alternate pattern is: 5 6 7
- The second alternate pattern is: 12 13 14
- The next number is part of the first alternate pattern.

There is a +1 counting pattern between alternate numbers.

5 12 **6** 13 **7** 14 **8**

Let's look at another question. Can you work out the answer?

36 21 31 25 26 29 [?]

A 33 B 30 C 28 D 21 E 23

The answer is: D (21).

How did you work it out?

−5 −5 −5

36 21 31 25 26 29 ?

+4 +4

- The sequence has a counting pattern. The first alternate numbers subtract 5.
  The second alternate numbers add 4.

LET'S PRACTISE!

In questions 1–7, find the number that continues the series in the best way.

Mark the correct answer in the box on the right.

1 3 6 9 12 [?]

A 11 B 25 C 15 D 9 E 20

2 22 9 26 12 30 15 [?]

A 18 B 33 C 35 D 34 E 20

3 2 4 8 16 32 [?]

A 6 B 64 C 48 D 16 E 62

4 5 10 15 20 [?]

A 24 B 26 C 25 D 30 E 35

5 9 8 9 11 8 14 8 [?]

A 7 B 9 C 18 D 22 E 17

6 33 27 29 28 25 [?]

A 29 B 26 C 19 D 27 E 21

7 64 63 64 62 64 61 64 [?]

A 64 B 62 C 59 D 60 E 63

Letters for Numbers

Word skills: number connections, logic and reasoning, addition, subtraction, division, multiplication

Letters for Numbers questions ask you to solve a letter calculation by swapping the letters with their given numbers.

We can see how the questions work by looking at some examples together. In this question, you will be adding and subtracting numbers but giving your answer as a letter.

Find out the answer to each letter calculation.

Choose the correct answer.

A = 16 B = 11 C = 9 D = 7 E = 18 — *letters and their corresponding numbers*

D + B + C − B = [?] — *missing number*

A B C D E

- First replace the letters with their given numbers: D + B + C − B = ?
  7 + 11 + 9 − 11 = ?

Working out the answer should be easy now!

- Start with the first two numbers: 7 + 11 = 18
- Next add 9 to 18: 18 + 9 = 27
- The last number is 11. We need to subtract 11 from 27: 27 − 11

7 + 11 + 9 − 11 = **16**

7 + 11 + 9 = 27 27 − 11 = **16**

Tip: Look out for questions where you are adding and subtracting the same number. They cancel each other out, which means we can take them both out of the calculation. In this example, we have +11 and −11.

Let's do one more question. See if you can work it out for yourself.

A = 35 B = 5 C = 4 D = 45 E = 10

B + E × C = [?]

A B C D E

The answer is: D (45).

How did you do it?

- First multiply 10 × 4 which is 40.
- Then add 5 to 40 to make a total of 45.
- 5 + (10 × 4) = 45

Tip: Remember! Work out division or multiplication before addition or subtraction.

LET'S PRACTISE!

In questions 1–7 the letters stand for numbers.

Find out the answer to each letter calculation.

Mark the correct answer in the box on the right.

1 A = 6 B = 8 C = 2 D = 12 E = 7

D – B + C = [?]

A B C D E

2 A = 15 B = 20 C = 30 D = 3 E = 10

E × D – B = [?]

A B C D E

3 A = 6 B = 18 C = 15 D = 5 E = 20

B ÷ A × D = [?]

A B C D E

4 A = 3 B = 2 C = 13 D = 5 E = 4

C – A – E – A = [?]

A B C D E

5 A = 36 B = 38 C = 20 D = 4 E = 2

A ÷ D × E + C = [?]

A B C D E

6 A = 20 B = 7 C = 3 D = 22 E = 4

C × B + E – C = [?]

A B C D E

7 A = 5 B = 3 C = 4 D = 6 E = 8

D × C ÷ B – A = [?]

A B C D E

Related Numbers

Word skills: number connections, logic and reasoning, addition, subtraction, division, multiplication

Related Numbers questions ask you to use the first two groups of numbers to find the number pattern that shows how all three numbers in a group are linked (related). You can then use the pattern or rule to find the missing middle number in the third group.

Let's walk through some examples.
In this question, look for the multiplication and division pattern.

In the question, **each** group has three numbers that are linked in the **same** way.

Find the number that completes the last group correctly.

Choose the correct answer.

(3 [4] 12)   (5 [6] 30)   (2 [?] 14)

three groups with three numbers linked in the same way

missing number to find

A 8   **B** 7   **C** 15   **D** 36   **E** 6

Look at how the numbers are linked in the first group: (3 [4] 12).

- Try different ways: 3 + 12 = 15; 12 – 3 = 9, 3 × 12 = 36; 12 ÷ 3 = 4.
- We can divide the third number by the first number to get 4: 12 ÷ 3 = 4.
- How many 3s are in 12? There are four: 3 × 4 = 12: (3 [4] 12).

Let's use the linking pattern with the second group of numbers: (5 [6] 30).

- Divide the third number by the first number: 30 ÷ 5 = 6.
- How many 5s are in 30? There are six: 5 × 6 = 30.
- Using the linking pattern, we can now find the missing middle number in the third group.

(2 [**7**] 14)

2 × **7** = 14   14 ÷ 2 = **7**

Here's another question to try by yourself.

(8 [3] 5)   (31 [10] 21)   (18 [?] 6)

A 24   **B** 3   **C** 13   **D** 2   **E** 12

Tip: Check your answer using an inverse calculation, eg 18 – 6 = 12 (12 + 6 = 18).

The answer is: E (12).

How did you do it?

- There is a subtraction pattern. Subtract the third number from the first number.
- First group: 8 – 5 = 3
  Second group: 31 – 21 = 10

LET'S PRACTISE!

In questions 1–8, **each** group has three numbers that are linked in the **same** way.

Find the number that completes the last group correctly.

Mark the correct answer in the box on the right.

1 (3 [6] 12) (5 [10] 20] (6 [?] 24)

A 9 B 2 C 8 D 12 E 4

2 (7 [21] 3) (8 [16] 2) (11 [?] 4)

A 15 B 44 C 7 D 40 E 41

3 (14 [17] 31) (34 [61] 95) (23 [?] 56)

A 33 B 79 C 32 D 46 E 34

4 (44 [66] 22) (26 [50] 24) (35 [?] 33)

A 2 B 38 C 68 D 39 E 67

5 (7 [1] 10) (5 [8] 15) (4 [?] 11)

A 4 B 2 C 5 D 3 E 6

6 (3 [9] 27) (4 [12] 36) (2 [?] 18)

A 15 B 9 C 16 D 6 E 20

7 (6 [7] 12) (4 [10] 13) (7 [?] 11)

A 6 B 5 C 18 D 4 E 13

8 (35 [46] 13) (67 [91] 26) (29 [?] 59)

A 88 B 86 C 78 D 80 E 30

Practice Test Paper

Information about this paper:

1. This paper is multiple choice. Mark the correct answer to each question in the box on the right next to each question. If you make a mistake, rub it out and try again.
2. Read all of the questions carefully.
3. You may find some of the questions difficult. If you get stuck, go to the next question. If you are not sure, choose the answer you think is best.
4. Work as quickly and as carefully as you can.

You have 25 minutes to complete this paper.

Do this practice test paper and mark your answers, look for any areas you can improve. This could mean you need to go back and look at a specific question type or work on getting quicker to do the questions in the given time. Keep practising!

In questions 1–4, find **two** words, one from each group, that are **closest in meaning**.

Mark **both** correct answers in the box on the right.

Example: (send label box) (store carton present)

A send X store

B label Y carton

C box Z present

Answer: **box carton**

Solution: Both **box** and **carton** are containers.

1 (cloth basic ornate) (colour patterned simple)

A cloth X colour

B basic Y patterned

C ornate Z simple

2 (water sail boat) (waves ship passenger)

A water X waves

B sail Y ship

C boat Z passenger

3 (leap crawl upward) (jump over frog)

A leap X jump

B crawl Y over

C upward Z frog

4 (collect pile rubbish) (tidy stones heap)

A collect X tidy

B pile Y stones

C rubbish Z heap

For questions 5–9, three of the four words are given in code.

One of the codes is missing. The number codes are **not** in the same order as the words.

Mark the correct answer in the box on the right.

REST	TEAR	FATE	SAFE
1365	6534	2315	

5 Find the code for the word **REST**.

A 4536 B 4326 C 1354 D 4365 E 4526

A B C D E

6 Find the word with the number code **1534**.

A TEAS B FEAR C AFAR D SEAT E STAR

A B C D E

7 Find the code for the word **AREA**.

A 3134 B 5362 C 5343 D 3453 E 3462

A B C D E

8 Find the word with the number code **4551**.

A TREE B FEET C REEF D TEES E SEER

A B C D E

9 Find the code for the word **RAFT**.

A 4316 B 4512 C 1565 D 6526 E 5325

A B C D E

In sentences 10–13, a **four-letter word** is hidden at the **end** of one word and the **start** of the next word.

Find the two words that contain the hidden word.

Mark the correct answers in the box on the right.

Example: Evan fed his hens and ducks.

Evan fed	fed his	his hens	hens and	and ducks.
A	B	C	D	E

A ☐ B ☐ C ☐ D ☒ E ☐

Answer: **hens and**

Solution: The hidden words is **sand**. Evan fed his hen**s** **and** ducks.

10 The wooden boxes were both empty.

The wooden	wooden boxes	boxes were	were both	both empty.
A	B	C	D	E

A ☐ B ☐ C ☐ D ☐ E ☐

11 Pour water into this metal kettle.

Pour water	water into	into this	this metal	metal kettle.
A	B	C	D	E

A ☐ B ☐ C ☐ D ☐ E ☐

12 The hikers wandered down the lane.

The hikers	hikers wandered	wandered down	down the	the lane.
A	B	C	D	E

A ☐ B ☐ C ☐ D ☐ E ☐

13 One huge talon grasped my shoulder.

One huge	huge talon	talon grasped	grasped my	my shoulder.
A	B	C	D	E

A ☐ B ☐ C ☐ D ☐ E ☐

In questions 14–18, three of the five words are connected.

Find the **two** words that are **not** linked with the three words.

Mark **both** correct answers in the box on the right.

Example: spring June summer April autumn

A spring B June C summer D April E autumn

Answer: **June** **April**

Solution: The three words spring, summer and autumn are seasons of the year.

The two words **June** and **April** are months of the year.

14 chart square graph circle triangle

A chart B square C graph D circle E triangle

15 next beneath under across below

A next B beneath C under D across E below

16 break mend smash shatter repair

A break B mend C smash D shatter E repair

17 scared nervous relaxed casual frightened

A scared B nervous C relaxed D casual E frightened

18 trunk forest branch twig wood

A trunk B forest C branch D twig E wood

In questions 19–23, the **same** letter must go into **both** sets of brackets.

The letter ends the word in front of the brackets and begins the word after the brackets.

Mark the correct answer in the box on the right.

Example: ba [?] ear fro [?] et

A t B b C m D g E y

Answer: **g**

Solution: The four words are ba**g**, **g**ear, fro**g**, **g**et. Only the letter 'g' can be added at the end and the beginning of all four words.

A B C D E

19 lea [?] age dam [?] oem

A w B p C s D f E c

A B C D E

20 to [?] olk ic [?] our

A y B f C e D t E p

A B C D E

21 num [?] ack gra [?] est

A w B t C b D n E s

A B C D E

22 stor [?] eat tri [?] ail

A h B e C k D p E m

A B C D E

23 rai [?] own bea [?] ust

A t B g C r D d E n

A B C D E

In questions 24–28, find the number that continues the series in the best way.

Mark the correct answer in the box on the right.

Example: 2 4 6 8 10 [?]

A 11 B 12 C 9 D 15 E 20

Answer: **12**

Solution: It is a sequence of even numbers. Count between each number to find a pattern.

24 13 17 21 25 [?]

A 29 B 27 C 28 D 23 E 30

25 4 8 16 32 [?]

A 48 B 24 C 64 D 40 E 128

26 88 80 73 67 62 [?]

A 56 B 58 C 60 D 59 E 54

27 67 60 64 57 60 53 [?]

A 44 B 60 C 51 D 46 E 55

28 37 42 40 45 43 48 [?]

A 46 B 53 C 44 D 51 E 52

---

29 Read the information below, then work out the answer to the question.

Mark the correct answer in the box on the right.

Ana, Owen, George, Hamid and Riya go out into the snow.

Ana, Owen and Hamid wear hats.

Hamid wears a scarf.

Riya wears her new scarf and hat.

Ana and George wear gloves.

Owen wears his scarf but no gloves.

Who wears the fewest items of clothing?

A Ana B Owen C George D Hamid E Riya

Answers

For extended answers and explanations, go to www.scholastic.co.uk/pass-your-11-plus/extras/gl

Word Meanings

Give it a Go!
(page 8)

words for angry	furious, mad, enraged, cross
weather words	rain, snow, wind, sun
types of walking	stroll, amble, march, hike

Similar Meaning
(page 11)

1	C	kind
2	A	ring
3	D	train
4	B	fly
5	C	lift
6	E	mirror
7	A	rock

Closest Meaning
(page 13)

1	A Z	angry cross
2	A Y	above over
3	A X	discuss debate
4	B Z	jewel gem
5	C Y	burn scorch
6	A Z	leap pounce

Opposite Meaning
(page 15)

1	B Z	victory defeat
2	A Y	tight loose
3	B Y	lift drop
4	C X	wild tame
5	B Z	wet dry
6	A X	combine separate

Two Odd Ones Out
(page 17)

1	B E	trip slip
2	A D	alert lively
3	C D	sand seaweed
4	B E	hat glove
5	C E	switch plug
6	A D	waterfall river
7	C E	colossal humongous

Word Connections
(page 19)

1	C Y	toe finger
2	B X	hot slow
3	A Z	fly float
4	A Y	volcano earthquake
5	C X	number colour
6	B Z	miserable jolly

Reading Comprehension

Give it a Go!
(page 21)

Meena joined the fewest clubs. She only joined the drama club.

Comprehension: True or Untrue?
(page 23)

1	D	Becky sometimes misses the school bus.
2	C	Leo likes vanilla ice cream.
3	E	Sushma likes tennis the most.

Comprehension: Most or Fewest?
(page 25)

1	A	Min
2	D	Thursday
3	C	Yasmeen

Making Words

Give it a Go!
(page 26)

create		
three-letter words	**four-letter words**	**five-letter words**
ace, act, arc, are, art, ate, car, cat, ear, eat, era, ere, rat, tar, tea, tee	acre, care, cart, race, rate, tear, tree	carat, crate, eater, erect, react, trace

Make a Word
(page 29)

1	A	wag
2	D	ten
3	B	note
4	E	clash
5	C	clap
6	D	beat
7	C	fit

Complete the Word
(page 31)

1	D	pea
2	C	coat
3	D	bow
4	E	art
5	C	task
6	A	luck
7	C	for

Insert a Letter
(page 33)

1	C	k
2	A	w
3	E	n
4	C	h
5	B	y
6	E	d
7	A	p

Move a Letter
(page 35)

1	E	y
2	A	a
3	D	s
4	E	g
5	B	r
6	D	c
7	B	r

Hidden Words
(page 37)

1	B	peat
2	C	gong
3	C	soft
4	B	skin
5	D	bowl
6	B	else
7	E	grab

Missing Words
(page 39)

1	A	ONE
2	B	OWN
3	C	EAR
4	B	ANT
5	A	MEN
6	E	ARE
7	A	CUT

Joining Words
(page 41)

1	C Y	rot ten
2	A Z	sail or
3	A Y	snow flake
4	A Y	book let
5	A X	spot less
6	B Z	pan cake

Codes

Give it a Go!
(page 43)

WORM = UQPO
FISH = DKQJ
CAMEL = ACKGJ

Letter Series
(page 45)

1	B	EV
2	D	IM
3	A	LK
4	E	TZ
5	C	KY
6	B	WH
7	D	YX

Letter Connections
(page 47)

1	C	OP
2	A	ST
3	E	WX
4	D	LR
5	C	TY
6	B	TG
7	A	XW

Related Words
(page 49)

1	B	DBS
2	D	LEAP
3	A	ZTCCB
4	C	DNJOC
5	E	JAM
6	B	MDPL
7	D	BROWN

Word Numbers Codes
(page 51)

1	B	5261
2	C	LESS
3	E	6431
4	A	SOLE
5	B	TOOL
6	D	6343

Maths Skills

Give it a Go!
(page 52)

	54		
	25	**29**	
11	**14**	15	
5	6	**8**	7

Complete the Calculation
(page 55)

1	C	3
2	D	12
3	B	8
4	C	6
5	E	6
6	D	14
7	A	2

Number Series
(page 57)

1	C	15
2	D	34
3	B	64
4	C	25
5	E	17
6	A	29
7	D	60

Letters for Numbers
(page 59)

1	A
2	E
3	C
4	A
5	B
6	D
7	B

Related Numbers
(page 61)

1	D	12
2	B	44
3	A	33
4	C	68
5	C	5
6	D	6
7	B	5
8	B	86

Practice Test Paper (pages 63–68)

1	B Z	basic simple
2	C Y	boat ship
3	A X	leap jump
4	B Z	pile heap

5	E	4526
6	B	FEAR
7	D	3453
8	C	REEF
9	A	4316

10	E	them
11	E	talk
12	B	swan
13	C	long

14	A C	chart graph
15	A D	next across
16	B E	mend repair
17	C D	relaxed casual
18	B E	forest wood

19	B	p
20	A	y
21	C	b
22	E	m
23	D	d

24	A	29
25	C	64
26	B	58
27	E	55
28	A	46
29	C	George